Maude Egerton Hine King

My Book of Songs and Sonnets

Maude Egerton Hine King

My Book of Songs and Sonnets

ISBN/EAN: 9783337007010

Printed in Europe, USA, Canada, Australia, Japan

Cover: Foto ©Thomas Meinert / pixelio.de

More available books at **www.hansebooks.com**

CONTENTS

POEMS OF LOVE AND LIFE

	PAGE
THE SAD LOVER,	3
LOVE AND LIFE,	5
ELSA,	7
LOVE'S TRAGEDIES,	9
TO HER INDIFFERENT LOVER,	11
LOSS IN SPRING,	13
THE KINGDOM OF THE CHILD,	15
TRANSFORMATION,	17
FORGIVEN SIN,	20
SPRING, IN FIELDS NEAR LONDON,	22
A MINOR POET AND LIFE,	24

BALLADS

THE BALLAD OF THE CRYSTAL BALL,	31
THE DEATH OF THE KNIGHT,	39

	PAGE
THE MAKING OF THE POET,	45
THE OLD KNIGHT,	49

SONNETS

'WHEN FATE, BLINDFOLD AND MOVED WE SEE NOT WHENCE,'	55
OUTSIDE,	56
'THE PITY OF IT! THAT THESE FOOLISH FEET,'	57
A YOUNG POET,	58
'TO STRIVE FOR GOOD AND SOMEWHAT TO ATTAIN,'	59

OUT OF DOORS

MORNING,	63
IN A GARDEN, EARLY,	64
YOUNG TREE IN SPRING,	67
BEFORE THE STORM,	69
A BREATH OF SPRING,	70
STATICÉ,	71
A SHADOW PICTURE,	76
A SUMMER NIGHT IN A DREAM,	78
ON THE DOWNS,	80

Contents vii

VARIA

	PAGE
A DREAM,	85
ALAS!	88
THE KING MEETS DEATH,	90
FATE AND THE DESPOT,	93
THE VEILED MAGICIAN,	94
ART TO THE WORLD,	98
VEGETARIANISM,	101

FROM OTHER LANDS

THE SHEPHERD'S PRAYER,	109
NIOBE,	110
ON THE PLATEAU,	112
ON THE MOSEL,	114

ERRATA

Page 3, last line, *for* smile. *read* smile.'
,, 25, line 10, *for* town *read* turn
,, 51, last line, *for* 'Twas *read* "'Twas
,, 111, line 2, *for* frailed *read* trailed
,, 113, line 8, *for* ask. *read* ask,

POEMS OF LOVE AND LIFE

THE SAD LOVER

(TO HIS LONG ABSENT MISTRESS)

WHERE stays my dear, and from what favoured bowers
    Makes wanton trial
Of one in joy and pain still faithful found?
  O goodlier than gold,
      More fresh than flowers,
  Come, for I grow so old,
And thou 'rt the only sun that backward round
    My dear life's dial
Can shift the shadow of my spended hours!

If pitying Fate my sadness to beguile
    Would send to me
My dove, my dear, I'd pray her 'Make a song
  Unto thy soothing lute
      A little while,
  And falling sometimes mute
In soft sweet pauses that to love belong,
    O bend to me,
And with kind kissing teach my lips to smile.

The Sad Lover

Come, my bright peace, and in thy bosom take
    And quite appease
This passion-haunted life, with summer breath
   Unseal my pent-up soul!
      Lest my heart ache
  Too long, and lose control.
And heart's desire in dreams, and dreams in death
    Seek desperate ease
Ere thy too tardy kindness come awake!

LOVE AND LIFE

WITH the first roses of the summer time
    Came Love and prayed for housing in my heart,
    But I would none of him, and bade him part,
Because the glamour of that golden prime
Haloed the hill of life I needs must climb,

And made me think, 'I need no company
    Save the ideal, that to a noble end
    Spurs my faint life: I seek nor love nor friend,'
It seemed so simple 'neath a summer sky,
Therefore to Love, 'I need thee not,' said I.

Now Winter shrouds the earth where Summer shone;
    The old ideal is still mine own,—as high
    And chill as those bright stars it bideth nigh,
And as I follow mutely, knoweth none
How my wild heart cries out, 'Alone! Alone!'

Love and Life

How my sad heart hath sought itself to fill
   With love and service of all souls—in vain!
   Still is there room to house a deathless pain
That sighs and murmurs, 'Come, O come, Love!' still,
'Once I opposed thee, take my broken will!

Kind Love, who treadest first the desert place,
   That the red blood-drops of thy tireless feet
   May bloom, for those who come, in roses sweet,
Whose tears bedew the dust of life with grace
Of healing springs in a parched wilderness;

Who riseth on a life, and straight behold!
   The heart, resistless, wings towards thy light
   As the sweet lark, that hath been mute all night,
Soars singing, when the gates of Day unfold,
Filled with new life of mystery untold,—

I want, I want thee, Love!' On adamant
   Of dead indifferent silence breaks my cry,
   And then I listen: 'twixt the earth and sky
Cometh no answer save the ghostly taunt
Of the weird echo, 'Love! I want! I want!'

ELSA

A soul in heaven looked down to earth,
    And sighed, 'So long have I waited here!
Hast forgot me, Elsa, amid the mirth
And the joy and strife
Of thy daily life?
    There is no heaven without thee, dear,
        Elsa, Elsa!'

The mother looked from the cottage door,
    And gazed with fear down the long dark
        lane;
'Art lingering, daughter, upon the shore?
My fond heart fears
For no star peers
    Through the night that's raving in wind and
        rain.
    Elsa! Elsa!'

Elsa

The sad old eyes will gaze in vain
    For many an hour of night and day,
Till they dim with a weight of age and pain.
For the old heart aches,
But the young heart breaks,
    And is fain to go home on that other way!
    Elsa! Elsa!

LOVE'S TRAGEDIES

O HEART of mine, and canst confess
    Unblushing, what hath raised thy fears?
Shame on thy loving foolishness!
One word less fond, one kiss the less,
    And must there even follow tears?

Love in that silly heart doth reign
    In tender tyranny o'er wit,
In little disappointment fain
To see a tragedy, and strain
    The possibilities of it!

Love is so sensitive of mood,
    He answereth to every breath,
He greets his mate in loverhood
And deems that all the earth is good,
    He bids farewell and dreams of death.

Love's Tragedies

Ofttime the heart that 's dear to him
    Hath kept him waiting ere it came,
Then all too soon his eyes will swim,
And all his joy in life grow dim,
    Before a fear he dare not name.

E'en in his rapture doth he cling
    The faster for his sudden fears,
Lest what he loves should spread its wing,
And all his sweetest smiles to spring
    From near about the fount of tears.

Prithee, good heart, I prithee school
    That hot inhabitant of thine
To cast out fear that would befool
Love's highest reason from its rule,
    And mar what else were nigh divine!

TO HER INDIFFERENT LOVER

There was a time, a time of yore,
   Death got me in his closing grip,
And drew me to a lonely shore
   To set me sailing in his ship;

When thro' that misty soundless place
   A cry, a cry rang in my ears,
And into mine there gazed a face,
   Too full of love's last dread for tears.

You would not then have cared to see
   The brightest eyes in all the earth,
For Death had claimed my poverty
   And turned it to an awful worth.

I felt love's hold upon the life,
   That drifted with the awful tide,
As in a dream I felt the strife
   Of love and death on either side.

To Her Indifferent Lover

A sudden flame of glad belief
   Leapt up, my fainting soul within;
If Death could wake so great a grief,
   What love, what love my life could win!

And so I turned and got a hold
   On health by just that slender thread.
And now the risen life is old,
   And common as our daily bread.

I could be brave to bear the pain,
   The deathlike drowse, the flash of fear,
Might I but fill your heart again,
   As then I filled it, dear, my dear.

LOSS IN SPRING

I HAD a hope this Spring would bring for me
   A gladness greater than the joy of Spring ;
Of all the Springs I hold in memory,
   Were none more lovely in their wakening,

More flushed with flowers, more mad in min-
     strelsies ;
   The birds all garrulous with golden wine
Thicken the happy tumult of the trees,
   Beneath whose slender shade the celandine

Mingles his sunshine with the daisies' snow
   In bladey grass, where greater blades betray
That hereabout when merry March winds blow,
   The daffodils are wont to have their day ;

The starry frolic of that golden crew
   Has vanished in a month of milder mood,
And pools and rills of wild-flowers shimmer through
   The gentle glory of the primrose wood ;

Loss in Spring

The common grass that glorifies the land,
   Thrilling with insect life, in joy receives
The soundless flood of light, the laurels stand
   Breaking its glory on a thousand leaves;

A breath from hidden violets wanders past,
   A sweet soul strayed from some forgotten tomb,
And like a happy dream come true at last
   The grey old fruit-tree stands in snowy bloom.

All, all is here, and lovely as of yore
   In resurrection beauty rich and rife.
Yet am I but an alien thing before
   The intolerably happy heart of life;

There lacks one tiny flower that once I thought
   Would crown all dreams, and hopes, and suffering.
For all her fulness Spring has only brought
   A sadness deeper than the joy of Spring.

THE KINGDOM OF THE CHILD

This glad, unthankful little one,
   Too young to know what wealth is his,
Doth a most mighty kingdom own,
   And mother-love that kingdom is:

A realm set round with high watch-towers,
   That joy may play, while love looks out,
A lawny garden full of flowers
   With sweet-briar hedges hemmed about!

His home is warm and lined with love
   And lavish mother ministries
Of heart and hand, beyond, above
   All seeming need, are ever his.

Across his childhood's golden day
   There steals no little cloudish mood,
But it is quickly sunned away
   By the kind eyes of motherhood.

The Kingdom of the Child

But one I know, a little child,
   And 'tis in truth a piteous thing,
For though so dear and undefiled
   The babe is but a banished king.

By all their names he strives to call
   The kindly faces daily seen,
But one name says he not at all,
   Nor can he guess what it may mean.

For from a mother's love so deep
   A piteous exile he, alas!
Her hands are folded in a sleep
   Beneath the daisies in the grass.

TRANSFORMATION

AFTER SEEING A CHRISTMAS FAIRY-PLAY PERFORMED
BY THE YOUNGER AND INFANT CLASSES
OF A LONDON BOARD SCHOOL

ARE these in truth the children of our city,
   These happy creatures dancing hand in hand?
Would that our love might keep them, love and pity,
   A little longer in this Fairyland!

How slow the school-hours seemed, how long the daytime
   To children's hearts with glad impatience filled,
And what a happy hubbub filled the play-time
   Of baby tongues in London street life shrilled!

Then, with the fog and lamp-shine, came a treading
   Of little feet down many a dismal stair,
And little companies went quickly threading
   The winding way with more than childish care.

Transformation

From noisome street, dull court, and unlit alley,
　With radiant faces came the chattering band,
For all they cared they trod the Happy Valley,
　For this one night were bound for Fairyland.

The School House reached, came rapid transformation
　To fairyhood from threadbare shabbiness,
And mutual wonder, wide-eyed admiration,
　Of each for other in the wondrous dress!

Some play as gentle-folk, and light and airy
　Shrill through the lordly rôles with Cockney tongue,
And there a very wan red-handed fairy
　Plays far too anxiously for one so young,

And 'infants' prove pathetically winning
　In elfin guise, half shy and wholly proud,—
And can this be the glad and good beginning
　That life distorts to form a London crowd?

O baby faces, dear, bright baby faces,
　Can we not keep you lovely as to-day,
Must work and want make havoc of your graces,
　And drink, their shadow, steal your souls away?

Transformation

O flowers, young flowers, and is there any pardon
    For social systems whose blind selfish stress
Thrusts out so many from life's happy garden
    To run to weed in a rank wilderness?

My thought has passed beyond your play and laughter,
    Dear boys and girls, to wonder, half afraid,
Shall we be proud and glad of you hereafter
    As in the happy citizens we made?

Or shall we shame to meet you where we drove you
    In soulless toil, and ignorant appetite,
And shall we have to know again and love you
    In reckless women trailing through the night?

In this dear crowd, these little lives and tender,
    I see the England that will one day be—
Ah me, her likely shame, her possible splendour
    Entangled with their unknown destiny!

FORGIVEN SIN

There was a righteous man who sinned one sin,
And humbled him 'fore God and wore him thin
   With prayer and fast to cleanse the single blot;
Then softly spake unto his soul within,
   ' Be comforted, sad soul, man knows it not;
   God hath forgiven, yea, He hath forgot.'

Then rose, made merry, seeing God forgave,
Amongst his sons and daughters bright and brave,
   And died in honour; nor did ever see
The spirits round that sin's forgotten grave,
   Nor how beneath their tears that fell so free
   That little seed was raised into a tree.

They shaped a cradle from its deadly wood
To hold his first-born's child; unseen they stood
   Watching the little life that knew no blame
Sap the dread poison in his healthy blood,
   That in his manhood brake in fiercest flame,
   And drove him for its fuel through shame to shame.

Forgiven Sin

He left a man-child in his place, and still
The spirits followed: naught for good or ill
   Was he,—mere ashes of his father's fire!
Moved by the mystery of an awful will
   They haunted like a fate that could not tire,
   And built his coffin from its branches dire.

Alone of all that race, one little child
Played in the meadows, glad and undefiled,
   Fresh as their flowers. They said 'the tale is told,'
And stirred the hearts of men, and made them wild
   For his young blood: 'His sires,' they said, 'of old
   Planted this tree now grown an hundred-fold;

It shades our land, it shuts out heaven's light,
We weary of the race and of the blight,
   Therefore he dies!' They found him in his glee,
And wreaked on him long ages of despite
   Who least deserved it, all too brutally,
   And crucified his body on the tree.

SPRING, IN FIELDS NEAR LONDON

Between the shining grass and cloudless sky
   I wandered dreaming, and about my ears
The innocent sounds of Spring fell pleasantly;
   I had no room for doubting or for fears,
For Nature charmed me to her own mild mood
   To fall in love with life and think it good.

Beyond the meadows, far away, there lay
   The great wide city, all its ugliness
And sin and sorrow on that lovely day
   Mistily shining in a bride-like dress;
And as I looked, the spirit of the Spring
   Stirred in my heart and made me wild to sing.

And then there passed me by a jaded man
   And tiny child, half-blinded in the heat,
Who scarce could walk where other children ran,
   But dragged with pain his little weary feet:
What hope was theirs, or to what aim they fared,
   One did not know, the other scarcely cared.

Spring, in Fields near London

Ah, how the sunlight died away for me,
   How all my happy dreaming and my songs
Were smitten with a frost!   One misery
   Out of all London's multitude of wrongs
Had put my pretty gift to bitter shame
   With the stern justice of its silent claim.

It cried, 'O Poets, filled with festal mirth
   Of Spring, remember in these golden hours
That winter still hath somewhere hold on earth,
   Withholding life, and love, and hope—fair flowers,
Fairer to God to whom they all belong
   Than these that move you easily to song.

Bring your lyres level with the patient woe
   Of these your slaves and bread-winners, and plead
With those who do not suffer, do not know:
   Then may be yours, one day to sing indeed
A Spring song worthy of a poet's breath,
   When love and life and hope have risen from
      death!'

A MINOR POET AND LIFE

He sings of Summer with her freight
    Of glories in the common grass,
While in the street and by his gate
    The wicked and the wretched pass.

At night he hears the far-off roar
    Of a great city's deep carouse,
Then must he rise and close his door,
    And enter deeper in his house.

Not his the power to feel and wrest
    A hope from out that unreined riot,
His heart might break within his breast,
    His songs would wait for happy quiet.

But though his walls shut out the din,
    He cannot find his peace apart,
For with him Life has entered in
    And draws him to her awful heart.

A Minor Poet and Life

He shrinks, and weeps, 'In vain, in vain,
   You haunt me early, haunt me late,
It is not mine to heal your pain,
   Nor make your need articulate!

Long time I wrestled with my art,
   To voice your passion: weak and wild
My words fell back upon my heart,
   The sobbings of a fretful child!'

What though the thoughts come free and thick,
   That town life's dust to faëry gold?
So many human souls are sick,
   And human bodies starved and cold;

What though his deep desire create
   A vision of the future good?
While all unloved and desolate,
   So many children cry for food?

He lays his scrip and feather by,
   And goes his way with hasty tread:
'The pretty useless gift may die
   If but these piteous babes be fed.'

A Minor Poet and Life

He labours with ideal desire
    Among the stricken multitude,
And warms his heart before the fire
    Of humble human gratitude;

He thinks the way once hard to find
    Lies here, in strife with want and sin.
A hint of Spring upon the wind
    Has touched his trembling heart within,

And stirs the sleeping mystery
    That is a joy, that is a pain:
'O song-bird, bidest thou yet with me,
    And art thou wild to out again?

Life's hold is heavy on the wing,
    Her moan has hushed thy happy trill;
Through all the banquet of the Spring
    Her skeleton will haunt us still!

Accursed is he will not fulfil
    His every chance of righting wrong,
Yet who can say a perfect will
    Would quench the smallest bird of song?'

A Minor Poet and Life

So, yielding to the double right,
   He works in shade, and sings in sun
To leave behind at fall of night
   A poem spoiled, a work half done.

BALLADS

THE BALLAD OF THE CRYSTAL BALL

WHAT brings, what brings ye, Lady May,
    To seek a hermit's lair?
The briar has torn your golden gown
    And ruffled your golden hair.

I care not for my golden gown
    Nor all the briars that be,
But for the power, ye wise old man,
    If ye would ye could give to me.

O I would give my lands, she said,
    To learn some cunning spell
Should shelter my love by day and night
    From sorrow and danger fell.

O I would give my life, she said,
    If ever this might be,
By water, by land, in life, or death
    There's nothing too hard for me!

The Ballad of the Crystal Ball

The hermit raised his bright old eyes,
    There needs no magic spell
To guard a knight of the holy host
    That's fighting the Infidel.

The lady brake a sweet briar-rose,
    And blushed a rosy red,
He's no whit further from merry England
    Than this little flow'r, she said.

I told him never gentle knight
    Let ladies plead in vain,
My heart will be broke in two, I said,
    Ere ever ye come again.

He would not stay for all my wrath,
    Nor yet for all my fears,
No words could stay him, but when I wept
    He stayed for my bright, bright tears.

No rite nor magic spell have I
    For Christian wife or maid,
This little crystal pure and bright
    Will lend ye a holier aid,

The Ballad of the Crystal Ball

And every night these three next nights
   God grant you a bright moon,
For there in vision lie perils three,
   And it's you must save him soon.

Once with speed of man and beast,
   And once with this world's pride,
And once by the power of prayer and fast
   And mighty great love beside.

And as ye hope for grace at last
   Ye shall not shrink nor fail,
Though it cost ye tears, and tears of blood
   To succour him from his bale.

Christ save thee, maid, the mother said,
   Where got so glad a look?
I've been away to the wood, mother,
   And sat me down by the brook;

I pulled the flowers that grew, mother,
   And heard a sweet bird sing—
I shall be a happy bride, mother,
   Before the swallows take wing!

The Ballad of the Crystal Ball

She watched the long day slowly die
   Within her maiden bower,
O quiet it was as any cell
   And pleasant as any flower.

She opes her lattice, bars the door,
   And trembles nigh to swoon;
Now, saints be praised, the lady said,
   That send me so bright a moon!

In the cool crystal depth she sees
   A ruined chapel stand
Where the roads cross, and five men lurk,—
   A wolfish and outlawed band.

She sees her knight, all light of heart,
   Along the lone road ride,
With never a thought of lurking death
   And never a squire beside.

Now up and wake, my brother dear,
   And make no noise nor stay,
I'll give ye a chain of fine red gold
   An ye reach my love ere day;

The Ballad of the Crystal Ball

Then ride and ride, my brother dear,
    As ne'er ye rode before,
And say there's death by the old cross-road,
    And death by the chapel door!

The second night she looked in
    I wis she wept for rage,
She saw her knight go by on foot
    Like a churl that sweats for wage;

She saw his brother, false Sir Hugh,
    Sit in his brother's seat
With the red wine in his brother's cup
    And his great hound at his feet.

Now, by my faith, the lady said,
    This thing shall ne'er befall;
Though I sell my land, and my milkwhite steed,
    I'll pay that false knight all.

Now wake, now wake, my pretty boy,
    And seek Sir Hugh of the Hill,
And bear this casket and little key
    And bid him to take his fill.

The Ballad of the Crystal Ball

And say I've gold and gold to spare,
    And more of gold I'll pay
Than ever my true knight had of him
    Ere ever the year's away.

Rise, little brother, and Christ me curse
    If ever I stint your wage!
I'll give ye my flow'ring red rose-tree
    And my bird in its golden cage;

I'll give the pretty toy of gold
    So long ye've craved and sore,
If only ye plead with false Sir Hugh
    As never ye pled before!

She took and kissed her crystal ball,
    O, dear above all price,
Ye've rescued my love from death and shame
    And will ye now save him thrice?

The third night came, nor moon nor star
    Looked through the heavy cloud:
Be silent, be still, ye silly heart,
    Why beat ye so quick and loud?

The Ballad of the Crystal Ball

Then slowly, slowly climbed the moon
    Behind the heavy skies:
I'll twist my hair with a silver pin
    Ere ever it veil mine eyes.

Then out and stepped the lady moon
    Shined in the crystal ball;
Be steady, be still, ye shaking hands,
    Or surely ye'll let it fall.

The first time that she looked therein
    She saw nor sign nor trace,
The second time she looked therein
    There gathered a mist apace,
The third time that she looked therein
    She looked on her own fair face.

The Lady looked and looked again,
    And stood there stony still;
But when the moon went in the cloud
    She laughed out sudden and shrill.

It frighted me, the lady said,
    A moment it shook me well!—
'Tis only a false, false magic, she said,
    That begins and ends in Hell!

The Ballad of the Crystal Ball

She dug a grave 'neath the red rose-tree
    And buried the crystal ball,
And never a look nor word gave she
    Of the harm that was worst of all.
But the roses died and the rose-tree drooped
    And withered before the fall.

THE DEATH OF THE KNIGHT

THE priest prayed loud by the bed-side
　　Though the sick man heeded him not,
And the doctor smoothed the pillow
　　And cooled the head that was hot,

And serfs in the sweat of the tillage,
　　And the household knaves, stood a-stare
At the man who had been their terror,
　　Now lying impotent there.

He lay and laughed in their faces,
　　Nor would own to the ghastly pain,
And he cried wild words, for the fever
　　Was high in the sick man's brain.

'Now leave me alone, Sir doctor,
　　I'll have neither your sweet nor sour,
For not with a wizard's physic
　　Will I lengthen my life one hour!

The Death of the Knight

How you plague me, priest, with your Latin;
    And as for the folk on high,
I could swear that they understand it
    No better than you or I!

For neither by prayer nor physic
    Can I ever again be whole,
For wine and women and warfare
    Have ruined me, body and soul!

O Saints! for a field and a skirmish
    And an axe swung deadly and well
In the hands of an honest foeman,
    And a headlong plunge into Hell!

To die in my bed like a burgher!
    How the Devil will grin and stare!
But in spite of you, priests and doctors,
    I'll die like a man, I swear.

Ho! gapers, go get me my armour
    And learn how a knight can die,
Tho' the breath be the last of my using
    I'll shout my old battle-cry.'

The Death of the Knight

They decked him out in his armour,
   And he lay in that grim mock state,
Though the weak old hands in the gauntlets
   Were helpless to lift their weight.

He lay and rambled and muttered
   Of the deeds he had wrought of old,
And of love and feasting and fighting
   And rapine and ill-got gold.

And ever anon delirious
   He would moan in his mortal pain,
And he cried wild words, for the fever
   Ran high in the sick man's brain.

'Thou mother of God, show pity!'
   Cried the pale and sorrowful priest;
'Is there ought that to do would save him
   Or soften his heart at least?

He cannot last for much longer,
   But he must not die in this state,
Or St. Peter and all the angels
   Will thrust him back from the Gate!

The Death of the Knight

As he spoke, the door was opened,
    And the sun broke in on the gloom,
And along with air and sunshine
    A child came into the room ;

Though born of a knave and scullion,
    There was never a rose more fair
Than the face with its eyes of wonder
    And haloed with sun-lit hair.

He saw the bright little maiden,
    And he stared and struggled to rise,
And the spirit was changed within him
    And glared through his haggard eyes ;

The lips that had mocked their pity
    With a blasphemy deep and wild,
Breathed low, with twitching of trouble,
    ' My God ! I forgot the child !

I must then have long been dreaming,
    For I thought ten winters ago
That they laid her beside her mother
    In a grave that was hid in snow.

The Death of the Knight

Yes, I thought that a long mound lay
    By a mound that was very small,
And that there I buried my heart—
    And was it a dream after all?'

For his thought went back in his madness
    To the one true love of his life,
And the two-fold grief he had stifled
    In a fury of sin and strife.

'Come hither,' the priest bade softly,
    And he lifted her up to him,
And she kissed the lips that were dying
    Till his eyes with tears grew dim.

And he said: 'God bless the maiden
    In her womanhood by and by.'
And he groaned: 'God save the maiden
    From such in the world as I!

If I *might* but live and protect her!—
    Come, doctor, quick! bring me your stuff;
If you save my life I promise
    You plenty of gold, enough

The Death of the Knight

To build a palace,—quick! saintling,
    Prithee, pray me the best of prayers,
To St. Hugo's Chapel I promise
    Two'—startled, the little child stares

To see the grey head fall forward,
    And they lift her down from the bed,
And they draw the curtain about him,
    Whose grim old spirit has fled.

THE MAKING OF THE POET

'Sing to me,' said God Apollo,
   God of Song, 'and be my priest.'
And the youth was fain to follow
   Such commands, and to the east
Turned and hymned his heart's first firer
And his golden-voiced inspirer.

'So! enough of hymns and praises,'
   Cried Apollo God of Song,
'And enough of stars, and daisies,
   Any bird my choir among
Sings the same! to give me pleasure
Thou must change thy tune and measure!'

Then he thought upon his Lady
   Till he thrilled in soul and sense,
And from out the leaf-land shady
   Sang of her sweet excellence,
So that all the roses, yearning
With the rapture, stood a-burning.

The Making of the Poet

Then the God Apollo rising
   Wrathful from his golden chair,
Cried, 'A little sound chastising
   Shall he have, that pipeth there
Songs for Shepherd-scenes the meeter,
Any swain sings thus, or sweeter!'

Earthward hast'ning then, he drove him
   From that happy summer ground,
Till the sky was dark above him
   And the wilderness around;
And because he could not make it
Pleasing, took his lyre and brake it.

Still he hunted him and haunted
   Over ways of stone and thorn,
Smote and bruised his heart, and taunted,
   Then, to make him most forlorn,
Sent, like frost upon a flower,
Death into his Lady's bower.

Cried Apollo, heavenward springing,
   'I have made him dumb as death!

The Making of the Poet

No more with his childish singing
   Will he waste his foolish breath.
Nor with songs of love-endearing
   Will he vex my sated hearing.'

Now when all the Gods in heaven
   And the earth below lay still,
Low! the midnight hush was riven
   With a sudden sound and shrill;
As from out of dreams that gladden,
One had waked to truths that madden.

And the sound brake into singing
   Like a passioned nightingale,
Up against the stars a-ringing,
   Till the wakened earth grew pale
At the sad and lovely fashion
That the singer told his passion.

Then Apollo woke, and hearing,
   Raised his godlike golden head,
Looked between the clouds, and peering,
   'Who doth sing so sweet?' he said,
And, because he thought he slew him,
Marvelled when he saw and knew him.

The Making of the Poet

There he stood, his hair's young golden
    Dragged with thorns and dank with dew,
Wan and wild his face and olden,
    Then the God Apollo knew,
Though the music had arisen
That the dart that oped its prison,

Pierced his heart, and lay there letting
    Throbbing life-blood fall with song;
And its hidden fiery fretting
    Made the music sad, and strong;
Till in tears of rapture glistening
Gods and men alike were listening.

THE OLD KNIGHT

THERE was a lady fair, and young, and wise:
A minstrel loved her, singing all his best
To wake a lovelight in her gentle eyes;
A poet made his passion manifest
In dainty scrip and sighs and sweet unrest;
And one could neither sing nor write, not he,
(For all so kind a smile her thanks expressed,
Which in his hungry heart he groaned to see,)
That grey old knight who loved her deep and silently.

Once in wild hope that sprang of his despair
He took the lute with eager hands ashake
And stole apart that none might see him there
And sighed, 'Ah, God! that these great hands
    might make
Some music for my dear, my lady's sake!'
And thereupon the strings did sudden smite:
O foolish fingers, that can only break
The prisoned music with such heavy might!
He cast the pieces down and laughed in wretched
    spite.

The Old Knight

And yet hope rose again, bidding him try
In such sweet sort to write, that her pure heart
Should take no harm of love breathed sad and shy
In courtly verse. In truth that was a part
God had not shaped him for, so little art
Had he to please a lady's dainty ears,
And win the highroad to her heart thereby!
Long time he strove to write his hopes, his fears,
Then left a blank page dabbled with his useless tears.

Twelve hopeless moons died out, then through the land
There ran a rumour soiling her fair name.
The bard was rhyming at a King's command,
The minstrel trod the road of waxing fame,
And gave no heed; but one grew hot with shame.
'I am not young enough to make delight
In song or verse for e'en the dearest dame,'
Said softly to himself that grey old knight,
'But not too old am I, I wis, to love and fight.'

The Old Knight

He went alone, and no soul knew he went,
And found the liar, and smote the mouth that
    lied,
And headlong into hell his soul he sent:
Yet as he slew, Death, still unsatisfied,
Reached out and gripped the victor in his pride,
Bursting the heart that beat so fierce and true.
And one that saw them fled to her and cried,
  'Lady, a stranger fought and overthrew
Thy lying foe, and fell beside the man he slew.'

And when they turned the cloth from off his
    face,
It shone as if it kept some sacred tryst;
They told their silent tale with knightly grace.
Those lips, nor she but only Death had kissed.
And, womanlike, the piteous truth she wist,
And in a sudden yearning bent her head
In hope of some faint pulse of heart or wrist;
And when they whispered, 'Nay, the man is
    dead!'
'Twas such an one as this I might have loved,' she
    said.

SONNETS

I

When Fate, blindfold and moved we see not whence,
    Smites greatest men, ofttimes they, disendowed
    Of common life's completeness, wander bowed
Through gates of loss to some large recompense;
As when, with passion and insight thrice intense,
    Blake's holy madness wrapped him from the crowd
    To show him heavens in hells, and there allowed
Sight of life's central fires: or, reft of sense
To outer noise, Beethoven clothed in sound
    All love, all loss, all life's supremest dower:
    Or Milton in his house of lasting night
With God and his great heart, there within found
    Large liberty and comfort, and the power
    Of prophet vision undistraught of sight.

II

OUTSIDE

Am I without the Church, O Lord of those
    Thy faithful souls, united in endeavour
    To keep Thy Spirit in their midst for ever,
And win away Thy kingdom from Thy foes?
To-night I strove to join the prayers that rose
    In sweet springs running in one Godward river,
    But some blind power still bade our spirits sever,
And held me coldly listening to the close.

I saw Thy people waiting faithfully,
   And a strange radiance dawning in each face,
   A deeper union with Thyself confessing,
And, mutely wondering what it all could be,
   So left them,—just the one in all that place
     That needing most, had somehow missed, a blessing.

III

THE pity of it! that these foolish feet
    That erstwhile kept the path should turn aside,
    That this sweet soul by genius dignified
Should forfeit late the crown of conquest, meet
For such white hair; that, bowed and incomplete,
    Should end this life, this life of patient pride,
    That seemed so strong, but could no longer bide
The stress of want and Fame's withholden sweet!
Better were death than this, unless e'en yet
    There be a hope we see not, a return
    In some lone prayer, or tears, or far-off call
May yet reach Love, that Love, who from his gate
    Seeks 'mid his nearing pilgrims to discern
    The feeble steps of his old prodigal.

IV

A YOUNG POET

Long since, in youthful insolence, I deemed
    The untried vigour of Spring in heart and brain
    The pledge of great fulfilment: glad and vain
I gazed where far-off mountain glory gleamed
Above a valley mist, and gazing, dreamed
    I too one day could join the laurelled train
    Upon the heights, whose thought and breath sustain
The soul of the world. O strange that it so seemed!

They dwell with stars and thunder; at their feet
I pluck the valley flowers, as is meet
    For one that housed such hopes and was so young,
For one, for all his love, could play no part
In their large life!—Yet cease not, poet-heart,
    Till such slight songs as lie in thee be sung.

V

To strive for good and somewhat to attain,
    To feel the daily footway tending higher,
    Till out the Past some long-thought dead desire
Renders by one all former footsteps vain,—
To worship noblest souls, and find a stain
    Suddenly slur the worship, to inspire
    Their kind belief, and bear the pitiless fire
Of undeservéd love,—to strive regain
The level of their steadfast pilgrimage,
    And know the unlessening space betwixt us, vast
    With forfeit opportunities of strife,—
These be our earnings, this Sin's bitter wage,
    The self-wrought fetter from the prison-past
    Marring the movement of repentant life.

OUT OF DOORS

MORNING

Then see, my rose, I open unto thee,
  That all impatient tappeth on the pane
  To call me forth, who dreaming long have lain,
To see how sweet a morning waits for me,
Where in the sun-smile, on the lawn there be
A myriad morning stars full tenderly
  Held in the tear-drops of a midnight rain.

IN A GARDEN, EARLY

If all the world had a pleasure-garden,
   And went there ever in early sun,
There were more to praise, there were less to pardon
   When the day is over and done.

There's an airy wisdom, a solemn lightness,
   A passion of power in brain and blood,
Belong to the dew and the still cool brightness
   When day is a flower in bud;

When half unconscious the heart is drinking
   At unseen fountains of life and faith,
And joy is wiser than deepest thinking
   In range of a rose's breath.

One lily I have, though late, still lifting
   Her cup with night-dew and fragrance fraught,
And pansies, ardent and dark, and drifting
   From dreamland to dreamy thought;

In a Garden, Early

The creeping fire of nasturtiums claiming
    Paling on paling of grey oak fence,
And reinless riot of marigolds flaming
    In merry magnificence!

My eager, innocent jasmine gazes
    Through a dainty tangle of leaf and gloom,
And the building hollyhock near by, raises
    Her spire with bloom over bloom,

And queens it over the thing beside her,
    The miss-grown sunflower, that droops and grieves
For her wizened face, and is fain to hide her
    In rank magnificent leaves.

I have phloxes silver and phloxes rosy,
    So sweet in service and glad to please,
With mines of wealth in their every posy
    For jolly bacchanal bees.

My poppies slenderly stemmed and petalled
    Hold cups of light to the young day's lips;
Save one, where a gossiping bumble settled,
    That bows and swings as he sips.

In a Garden, Early

On a lush lawn with its blinking daisies
    And gleaming quiet, a soul may think
Of the wealth of life, till its unsung praises
    Will fill the heart to its brink!

And aspiration grows nigh believing,
    And life's best chapter is just begun,
And there's ne'er high aim that's beyond achieving
    In sight of the early sun;

And prayer soars up like a bird above me
    At thought of a garden, that still extends
With the number of human hearts that love me,
    And love that I feel for friends;

And I and the world grow young together,
    And feel good whether we laugh or pray:
And now, come sunny or cloudy weather,
    I've had the best of the day!

YOUNG TREE IN SPRING

O SKY, you know me? I am come again
    Out of a bare black sleep!
Sun-summons, wash of wind and thrill of rain
Beat on the doors fast closed, but all in vain,
    For life that lies too deep
For any frost, will rise a bidden guest
    At Spring's glad festival!
Without a dream my soul lay lost in rest,
    Till, at that touch and call,
I grew aware of life, an inner fire
    Of memory and belief
Ran upwards, outwards, in a great desire,
    And lo! then leaf by leaf,
Remembering my other springs, I rose;
And earth around remembers too, and grows
    Into her ancient grace,
With ' Here were my daisies—there before it froze
    A tiny rill did race.'
The wild young wind that ever caught me so
    Still takes me at his will,—
The dark sweet violet, still hiding low,
And over the hedge in golden dance and glow
    The jocund daffodil,—

Young Tree in Spring

The bird that in my budding branches sings,
    The happy, happy bird,
A creature careless, being blessed with wings,
How far a-field his mid-air foothold swings
    By random breezes stirred,
Voice of that passion of life that moves in me
To a mute growth of glory,—the first bee
    Crooning in early shine
Round risen buds, dear in his memory
    As a deep honey-mine,
All the quaint gladness Spring did ever yield
To frolic lambs in daffodilly field,—
    The woodlands living peace
Of hourly growth, and gentle lives unsealed
    In revels of release,—
All, all are here, and Spring fulfils her troth,
And here the happy pain, and gladness both
    That bring me a bud's birth,
And thy warm hold on my wild tiptoe growth
    O Earth, dear Earth, dear Earth!
The wind, the wind in my hair, the passing wing,
    The beat of sunwarmed rain,
The joy of life, the hope of another Spring,
    Are mine, they are mine again!

BEFORE THE STORM

ONE moment since and every living thing
    Seemed as if held beneath a charm of death,
The trees, then moveless, now wake shuddering,
Putting up leaves all pale and sick with pain,
As if in prayer for the dear freshening rain,
    With trembling hope before the creeping breath.

In silence that foretells the coming sound,
    Above, the grey clouds grope through the grey space,
Slowly, but on one mighty purpose bound,
Like blindfold giants, each one feeling forth
For the blind foe, to test the awful worth
    Of might and might, in one immense embrace.

Now is the languid air perforce astir
    Before the wingéd storm that hastens on,
And one late bird, poor startled voyager,
Hastes to the leafage where his housèd mate
Warns shrill and sudden him she doth await
    In the glad tree now fiercely bent and blown !

A BREATH OF SPRING

O BLESSED time of all things gay and green !
   Adown a sunray slips a showeret clear,
And twigs and stalks and barest things are seen,
   To bud beneath the young sun of the year.

And on the hill a light wind is at play,
   Brushing the young-eyed daisies with his wings,
And far above the dear earth in her May,
   A soaring laverock sings, and sings, and sings.

STATICÉ

There is a garden far away,
   Where Joy and I have walked together,
My heart is with it all the day,
   My heart is there this dear June weather,

Is in a flower that's fraught for me
   With magic in its every petal,
While others pass, or smile to see
   That e'er a bee should care to settle;

Of all its hundred eyes no eye
   Will open to a cloudy heaven,
Nay, you would pass my Staticé
   To see how some near rose had thriven!

But if a morning should arise
   Upon the earth in broad bright splendour,
And all the land be full of eyes
   And sounds of waking bright and tender,

Staticé

And the white dews that glorify
    Mount all too soon the golden ladder,
And lark on high and mavis nigh
    Strive each to make a glad world gladder,

And like a fitful sigh the breeze
    Scarce stir the golden robe of morning,
And all things in their own degrees
    Be bent upon their own adorning,—

Then out and speaks my Staticé,
    'The day is worthy of my beauty,
And many a butterfly and bee
    Are here to love and do me duty,

A thousand little things there be
    That long to sip and store my sweetness,
A broad bright sun to shine on me
    And call me forth in all completeness.'

She opens all her guest-rooms wide
    For many and fast the folk are coming,
And soon the bush on every side
    Is loud with happy creatures humming.

Staticé

O Staticé, how proud you are!
   You give without or stint or measure:
Of all your stars no honey-star
   Is closed upon your golden treasure,
A myriad bees may bear it far
   To give a far-off people pleasure!

So as I see you in the blaze
   With heat and humming all a-quiver,
The rapture of the best of days
   Is what you mean to me for ever.

Last night I dreamt the world went wrong,
   The heart I treasured 'scaped my keeping:
I thought my life had sung its song,
   And chill and mute I wandered weeping;

While as I roamed I heard the sound
   Of bees at work; with threefold power
Beat my fond heart, for looking round
   I spied my Staticé in flower,

With every star wide-spread and loud,
   With noises of a winged miner,
'Ah, see!' I cried through tears, 'the cloud
   Is surely past, the day is finer':

Statice

I thought my heart would break in two
   With the wild hope the flower gave me,
'O heart!' I wept, 'he must be true,
   And God has sent the flower to save me!

'For Staticé will bear no part
   Save in the best of happy weather!'
For in my dream it seemed my heart
   And Staticé were bound together.

I never saw the flower save there
   In the dear garden far-off yonder,
And once within that dreamland where
   I never any more may wander.

But, O if thou wouldst grow, delight,
   Within my little city garden,
I'd water thee with tears as bright
   As angels weep in love and pardon:

I would uphold thy stem that none
   Of summer's winds would break or flout thee,
And pray to God to send the sun
   And bring the happy bees about thee.

Staticé

O Staticé, my Staticé!
   The year is in its June-tide beauty,
And butterfly and bee and I
   Are here to do you loving duty;

Dear Staticé! some hearts can break
   Though June's own sun of suns is beaming;
O come and give me while awake
   The happy hope you gave me dreaming!

A SHADOW PICTURE

Across my blind when I awoke at day
  A lovely shadow lay,

A few belated leaves upon a trail
  Of creeper, fine and frail,

Whose every tiny tendril gave delight
  In my sun-picture bright;

Then by the coming of a shadow-bird
  The shadow-trail was stirred,

That for a moment's rest alighted there
  Midway in golden air,

And in the breeze that swung the trail aside,
  It plumed its wings out wide,

A Shadow Picture

And had no fear, for all its hold was frail,
  To swing with the shadow trail.

Heart and bird and trail danced, all aware
  That life was glad and fair,

Yet but a while,—I saw the tiny breast
  Swell with a glad unrest,

And then a happy flutter, and a flight,—
  A shadow lost in light.

A SUMMER NIGHT IN A DREAM

I PASS in a rapture of wonder
   Through gardens grown vasty and strange;
All about and above me and under
   Is touched with a terror of change.

I know I am dreaming, that never
   On earth lay such shadow and gleam,
And I fear lest a whisper should sever
   The barely closed doors of my dream.

The gardens lie dreamy and stilly
   'Neath night at her languorous noon,
And many a tremulous lily,
   Is breathing her scent to the moon.

And poppy, the silver-leaved sleeper,
   Is silently thrilling with bliss,
And I feel that her crimson grows deeper
   For the dew and its delicate kiss.

A Summer Night in a Dream

On the deep-breathing breast of the river
   The lilies all languidly lie,
And ever they dreamily shiver,
   As the ghost of a breeze wanders by.

'Mid the scent of its own heavy blossom
   The tree doth deliciously dream,
Soft shedding its bloom on the bosom
   Of the leisurely, lily-leaved stream.

The rose drooping low in her beauty
   Is white as the mantle of death,
And the breeze to her charms doeth duty
   And draws in his worshipping breath.

The stars a sweet music are making,
   But their voices are veiled in the height
And only a heart-throb is breaking
   The passionate hush of the night.

ON THE DOWNS

We climb and climb this sunny day
Until 'the height is near!' we say,
    And gaining that, we find the summit
Still leans in leisurely slope away.

Too oft life's repetition kills
A treasured dream,—this day fulfils
    The prophecy of my rich remembrance
Of childish pleasure on these dear hills.

Blue butterflies, my old delight,
Still seem for me, in flickering flight
    About the hare-bells, hare-bells wingéd,—
The hill-snail tiny and brown and white

Still finds the pasture to his mind,
And trembling spear-grass throws a kind
    Of bloomy pallor o'er the greensward,
And ever a little random wind

On the Downs

Wakes whispers in the tufted ling,
And bids the browsing bumble cling
    The closer for his scabious nodding,
And sets the thistledown scampering.

The coombe is climbed, and from the crown
I see the sheltered red-roofed town,
    My brain is clear as air and sunlight,
My heart is light as the thistledown.

O peace and soft simplicity
Of grassy hills! with ne'er a tree,
    Save one old thorn long wrought and writhen
By shoreward winds from a fierce salt sea,

And here, high up in hills and bare,
A happy valley, nothing there
    Save thymy scent and sloping sheep-track
And grass and silence and golden air!

And ever if the wind be still
A single sheep-bell comes to fill
    The sunwarmed lull,—at happy leisure
The sheep and shepherd come up the hill.

On the Downs

The sheep draw near, I hear their feet,
I hear them tug the turf they eat;
    No head is lifted, save in passing,
All grave and greedy, from sweet to sweet.

And now again the day's broad bloom
Grows graver in the gentle gloom
    Of clouds that pass, whose shifting shadows
Sweep slow and softly from crown to coombe.

To that large flight my eyes respond
And turn my charmed thought vagabond
    Beyond the town, the valley homesteads,
The hills around them, the hills beyond,

To seek the crown of all for me,
Where, in that silver mystery
    Between the farthest hill and heaven
My eager fancy would find the sea.

VARIA

A DREAM

I

I saw a field whose grass was full of flowers,
   Red roses, daffodils, and lilies, all
   The wealth of all the seasons come at call
Of some weird spirit strong in stolen powers.
   And there amid that flowery festival,

And 'neath the rainless blue, stood one whose face
   Excelled all flowers. But when she moved, from out
   That forest of fair growths, a swinish rout
Ran grunting after, leaving brutal trace
   In broken stems and petals strewn about.

II

I saw her once again, grown old, accurst,
   Heard her, while weaving at her noiseless loom
   The webs that tangle souls in silken doom,
Croon in her cool dim hall the song that erst
   Guided her creatures to that palace tomb.

A Dream

And at her feet her wretched captives lay,
   Shadowy, sick of thrall, yet without might
   To rid them of it; 'twas a piteous sight
To see a man's soul in a beast's eye pray
   For manhood withered by her hellish rite.

But Circe had grown blind, she could not see
   The silent revelation in those eyes
   That told, her ancient power and witcheries
Could bind, but please no longer; and that she,
   Once fairest, had grown foulest in her guise.

The witch of all the world was blind, and yet
   Their trouble dawned on her: perchance a sigh
   Stole to her ear, wherein she might descry
The pain of creatures who can ne'er forget
   The forfeit life God meant to be so high,

For the blind fingers trembled, and a wave
   Of proud half-pity crossed the ruined face;
   She stayed her weaving, and a little space
It seemed to me her thought was in the grave
   Of her far past, seeking some sign or trace

A Dream

Of what might yet reverse their doom,—in vain !
    The foolish fingers trembling o'er the thread
    Had lost their way ; it broke, and overhead
A face flashed out, and into dark again
    For evermore ; Mnemosyne had fled.

No love to hold, no power to bid them rise
    From hated thrall ! Slowly she rose, nor spoke
    While God's whole meaning on her spirit broke,
Then sudden with frenzied hands beat her blind
      eyes
And shrieked!——
                And in that horror I awoke.

ALAS!

A LITTLE thought of doubtful kin
Came housed himself my heart within,

And spied about, and furled his wings,
And tried my heart's long silent strings,

And to the sound he wakened there,
I sang a song upon the air;

A song, and songs, and ever more,
I never sang so sweet before:

Until a whisper came and stayed
The sweetest songs I ever made,

And told me, 'twas a very sin
Had made himself so snug within!

Alas!

And so I took that busy sprite,
That was my helper and delight,

And drove him far before my fears,
And cleansed his dwelling with my tears.

But since I turned him out of door,
I sing my happy songs no more.

THE KING MEETS DEATH

'About this time the King fell ill of a grievous sickness, so that the physician could give him no hope of his life beyond the space of a twelvemonth. From that day onwards, as his sufferings waxed greater, there grew along with them a patience and a sort of gracious gladness, and such store of wise counsels as made men think God had brought him into affliction to show him truths not else to be attained, for the cheer of his own soul and the bettering of his people.'—*The Chronicle of a Little Kingdom.*

A HAND hath led me to life's very edge;
   Into two worlds I look, two kingdoms see,
And linger 'neath the tragic privilege
     Of moving men by that high mastery
     That only death-in-life could give to me.

A wisdom not mine own informs my brain
   A greater Love hath made my heart his shrine,
A greater Spirit chose me in my pain
     To be his oracle; and makes it mine
     In human words to clothe a thought divine.

The King meets Death

Might I but keep my Kingship under God
    Long years of pain were sweeter than all ease !
This may not be, my feet have long been shod
    For the last road ; yet ere the great release
    I would reveal the Angel of my peace.

There is a power that nerves all noblest strife,
    And yet men strive to thrust it out of door ;
A hope as old as death, as wide as life,
    That I, too, held too good for truth of yore :
    Death proves my soul to me, I doubt no more.

Into the dark I went, into the dark,
    With world-wise heart and ever-failing frame,
But in my soul I bore that tiny spark
    Which Death's wide wings fanned to so bright a flame,
    Whither I went I knew and whence I came.

Now can I bear all burdens, grown so wise,—
    Even this load of pain, whose growing weight
Drags me away from arms that agonise
    To hold me, and the thousand ties of state
    Entangled with my one poor human fate,—

The King meets Death

With steadfast joy, till passes into dust
    The painful shell that gave me housing here,
And I, beyond all touch of worm or rust,
      Bid ' Farewell Death, thou couldst not spoil my cheer,—
    Thy work is with the dust: how should I fear?'

FATE AND THE DESPOT

'Not this, not this, but these!' I cried
 In my power and pride;
'Do you dream, that whether for good or ill,
'Twill pass the barriers of my will?
Sooner, I'll yield my throne and treasure
Than this small thing that I love 'yond measure!'
 (So I cried as the shade came creeping.)

'Not these, not these, but this!' cried Fate,
 And she passed my gate,
And she left my treasure, the courtier-crowd
That loathed in secret and praised aloud,
My heavy crown, and my mighty throne,
And my myriad slaves,—but she left me alone,
For she swept me by and becked on death
 With his blasting breath,
And sought and found the poor pale thing
I loved, I loved! then with wide-spread wing
 She left me, the great king, weeping.

THE VEILED MAGICIAN

A DREAM

Have you heard, O have you heard
  Of a music bright and sad,
    That has made a wise world mad
      With its sorrow and its mirth,
Coming from no singing bird
  But a spirit void of grace,
    Whose strange song and veiléd face
      Have a deathless power on earth?

If you listen, if you look,
  You will see the curious thing,
    You will hear the creature sing
      As he treads by night and day
Through the forest, by the brook,
  Up the mountain—anywhere,—
    If a living thing be there
      He will surely pass that way.

The Veiled Magician

You will see the strangest sight;
  Here a maid in summer grace
  Breaking from the love-embrace,
    Fascinated by the thing
That has robbed her of delight,
  Or a little lamb behold
  Fleeing from the shelt'ring fold
    Just to die in following;

Here a King who in the height
  Of a revel glad and sweet,
  Heard the strange mysterious feet
    Treading by his palace-gate,
Heard, and went out into night,
  Hid his glory in the throng
  Following the creature's song,
    Never more to separate.

So they follow one who goes
  With an ever hidden face,
  Each one dropping in his place,
    While he doth not heed or save
From the day's dawn to its close;
  Child and lamb and wise man fall,
  And the ending of them all
    Is the silence of the grave.

The Veiled Magician

What a crazy crew it is!
  One and all have turned aside
  From a flow'r-set path and wide,
    Just because an unknown voice
Calls them to the wilderness,
  Where they strive with foes in fight
  That had never met their sight
    But for this their foolish choice!

What the motive of their strife?
  They have earned no word of grace,
  Nor have ever seen the face
    That a wise world holds accurst;
They have lavished all their life
  On a foolishness of faith,
  And are going down to death
    No whit wiser than at first!

Will the Spirit ever tread
  Even till the very birth
  Of the last day of the Earth?
    Will he turn him then and say
Which of all the quick and dead
  Faithfullest have followed him;
  Even while their eyes were dim
    With the sorrows of his way?

The Veiled Magician

Will he sing his song again,
   And the dead who held it dear
   Rise again in joy to hear
     From their chill and silent place?
Will the veil be lifted then
   And the brave who would not borrow
   Help of hope to bear the sorrow
     Learn his name and see his face?

ART TO THE WORLD

Hither, O weary and dusty feet,
Steal softly away from the city street
Where strife is endless tho' life be fleet,
   And failure findeth nor pity nor pardon;
   Come, wander away to my great green garden
Where flowers are eternal and ways are sweet.

Like dead leaves swept by a wingéd wind
They rush to their work at the wheels that grind,
And forge them links of the chains that bind,
   The blood and the sweat and the tears are falling,
   And I in their midst am calling, calling,
To the crowd that passes me deafly, blind.

Their blood is hot for the gaudy gold,
The spirit within is quiet and cold
As a seed asleep in the winter mould;
   They wrestle and run for the highest places,
   The sweat and the tears run down their faces,
They lose or gain, and the tale is told.

Art to the World

Hither! for you, O heedless throng,
I have kept the blossoms the year along
And gathered all summers to serve my song;
   I have holy tears for the eyes that weep not,
   And slumber songs for the eyes that sleep not,
And the sword of God for the ruling wrong.

I would open your heart to subtle grace
In things uncomely and counted base
By the coarse crowd in its common race;
   I would touch your dreaming with starry beauty,
   And flower the path of your waking duty,
I would soften and strengthen and bend and brace.

I know the truth through its varying dress,
And soar where Science must stoop to guess,—
And the day that's coming will once confess
   Mine were no visions of idle dreaming,
   But songs of a sunrise of brighter beaming,
And then it will know me and love and bless,—

The blossoms of life she is fain to mar,
As petal by petal she drives afar

Art to the World

The truth and the beauty that in them are,
   Whiles I, I leap to the great stars shining
   And grasp them, close to my broad brow twining
The song and the secret of star and star;

Then leave their beautiful noise behind
The higher silence to seek and find,
Where bird ne'er sang nor a star hath shined,
   Till ever the pathless way ascending
   I gasp in an ocean of space unending
That deafens and drenches and strikes me blind.

Blind, but with heart athirst for the true,
With passionate pinions I beat the blue
And bruise till eternity's self breaks through;
   My heart throbs in through the sky-roof riven,
   A heart hath answered me out of heaven,
And gives me the secret of life for you!

Oh slaves and seekers, the time is fleet,
Hither with weary and dusty feet
Steal softly away from the loveless street
   That holds nor pity nor peace nor pardon,
   Oh wander away to my great green garden
Where flowers are eternal and ways are sweet!

VEGETARIANISM

(DEDICATED TO A VERY GENTLE FRIEND)

When I tell how sad a thing
   Wears my heart out year by year,
Sight of creatures suffering,
   Martyrdoms of service here,

Seldom paying wrong for wrong,
   Dumb before a human rage,
Toiling hard and toiling long
   To be slain in useless age,

Never sacred from abuse,
   While a breath of helpless life
Holds them fit for slavish use,
   Or for science with her knife,

You will never ask again
   Why I made my vow, and chose
Ne'er to add by death or pain
   To a cup that overflows.

Vegetarianism

See the little god of self,
    Custom waiting on his greed;
Craves he feast of flesh or pelf,
    All is sanctioned by his need.

Ceaseless toil of men and beasts
    Is his worship's heavy price;
And the cities teem with priests
    Slaying hourly sacrifice.

No such load of death and toil
    Can my single life redress,
But at least I need not spoil
    Any live thing's happiness.

They that round about me live,
    Watchful love and housing earn,
And the creatures ever give
    Kindly service in return:

Things that with their shy sweet life
    Make the woodland breathe and thrill,
Know there's ne'er a shade of strife
    'Twixt their pleasure and my will.

Vegetarianism

So, because I prize the worth
    Of all life and liberty,
One small corner of the earth
    Shall be glad because of me.

You with other faith than mine
    Ask me how I break my fast,
How I sup and how I dine?
    Come and share my sweet repast.

There's a nest among the straw
    In the barn-end out of sight,
There this morn I peeped and saw,
    Where the eggs lay warm and white.

Since the homely creatures thrive
    After sharing sweets with me,
Take we these, and from the hive
    Harvest of the honey bee:

Milk from cows serenely grave
    With a weight of meadow lore,
Who at evening lowing crave
    Riddance of their creamy store.

Vegetarianism

Or unearth a sweet hard root,
    If thy hunger make thee fain;
Cull the clustering bramble fruit,
    Sweet with sun and swelled with rain.

Bring me lettuce, crispy, cool,
    Crystal salt and sweetest bread,
Then a rosy apple pull
    From the mossed bough overhead;

In the nutwood bend and search
    Boughs the sun comes glinting through,
Tell the squirrel on his perch,
    There be nuts enough for two!

Oak and elm boughs interlaced
    Yonder shade my sobbing spring:
Stoop and cup your palm and taste
    Liquid song and icy sting;

'Tis a draught that never turns
    Foolish brains, or lights within
Feeble hearts a fire that burns
    For a sacrifice of sin.

Vegetarianism

Leave we now the quivering heat,
    Spread our feast and there carouse,
Where the grass is cool and sweet
    'Neath the apple-burden'd boughs.

Laverock, keep thy fiery bliss,
    Soaring song and liberty;
God shall never mourn nor miss
    One of all His choir for me.

Thou, who deem'st thy life as good,
    Though God made thee not to sing,
Farmyard mother, with thy brood
    Warm and cheeping 'neath thy wing,

Rabbit, with thy merry rout,
    In the warren near the farm,—
Thou wouldst make a zealot doubt,
    With thy rapine and thy harm!—

Who, whene'er I softly near
    Shew'st me, as thou see'st me stand,
Flash of tail, and flick of ear,
    And a round hole in the sand,

Vegetarianism

Deep-voiced mother in the field,
    Where thy lambkin plays and thrives,
God hath set no other shield
    Than our love around your lives :

Come about us, feel no fear,
    While we eat and take our rest ;
Ne'er a creature suffered here
    In my banquet of the best.

FROM OTHER LANDS

THE SHEPHERD'S PRAYER

(ARENA CHAPEL, PADUA)

Dear Lord, who of Thy love hast lent to me
   This power of art,—whereof, I pray Thee, hold
The springs for evermore, nor let it be
   Mine own, lest gratitude to Thee grow cold,
And so I put it to mere human use,
Which in Thine eyes could only be abuse,—

Be with me now and guide this faithful hand
   In Thine own lines ; O use me as a glass,
To mirror forth the way that Thou hast planned
   For men's salvation, even if it pass
Above my ken : make fair mine art to shew
The King in all His beauty, till men know,

To be His servants as their sires have been,
   Is best. O Shepherd, I have drunken deep
Of Thy still waters, in Thy pastures green,
   And yearn in love for these, Thy other sheep,
To lead them thither from the World-wolf's den !
To that end, guide my heart and hand. Amen.

NIOBE

(FLORENCE)

They were so gloriously fair,
I found no beauty anywhere

So grand as that which glorified
My Motherhood!—I cast my pride

Against the very Gods; alas,
The poor proud mother that I was!

The Gods in silent anger burned,
And over night my fate they turned,

And came and smote with blasting breath
My loves, my darlings unto death.

And on through all the lonely years
I see their laughter through my tears.

*   *   *   *   *

Niobe

In Athens, while her Golden Day
In sunset splendour frailed away,—

Whose beauty, waxing soft and free,
Cast off its stern divinity,

Whose porches rang with foolish breath,
Her godsent teachers dumb in death,

Whose cultured revels set a prize
Before barbaric envious eyes,

The while she dreamed her little state
Could face the world confederate,

And made her boast, tho' all the air
Grew thick with doom,—in deep despair.

One wrought all these and fashioned me,
And gave the name of Niobe,

Though, while his heart in secret bled,
'This is my stricken land,' he said,
'These are her glories dying, dead.'

ON THE PLATEAU

The blue-bloused peasant gathers grain
   That floods the valley-depth with gold,
But on this high up-lifted plain,
   The lingering cold

Withholds what scanty summer grace
   The earth untended strives to bear;
One kindly human-hearted trace
   We welcome there;

A tiny hut and all alone,
   No sign of housèd life in sight,
And won from wastes of weed and stone
   A garden bright.

In chilly silence seldom stirred
   The land around lies flat and bare,
With ne'er a tree for weary bird
   To shelter there;

On the Plateau

But in the precious garden space
   A grain-decked box upon a pole
Betrays our hermit's heart of grace
   And gentle soul.

Whoe'er the solitary be
   Helps God about His gracious task,
And feeds the feathered family
   That may not ask.

He gains three gifts will sure amend
   Some lack in that lone life above,
A little song, a little friend,
   A heart of love.

ON THE MOSEL

Between high hills the river windeth on,
    Here, laving their sheer pedestals of rock ;
There, 'twixt the mountains and its rapid run,
    A little chapel shepherding a flock

Of humble homes, o'erlooks the dust-white road,
    Where with loud whip the blue-bloused peasant drives
His mild strong oxen ; bearing a like load
    Both man and beast wear out their lowly lives.

And round the homes sweet lawny levels lie,
    Shady with fruit-trees, green with mountain rills,
And there beyond, stands dark against the sky,
    The pathos of the labour-mantled hills,

Whose every ledge and crag is clad in vines
    From out the rock with brave toil hardly won,
That now await amid their tiny shrines
    In earnest patience for the ripening sun.

On the Mosel

See, the clouds break! one moving gleam of light
    Passes in blessing, on from hill to hill,
Beyond the lonely peak where day and night
    Our Lady of the Vineyard watches still.

Life hardly earned, tired peace, and little play,
    Then the long rest when God will give the dream!
And through it all the river runs away
    To a far city and a larger stream.

www.ingramcontent.com/pod-product-compliance
Lightning Source LLC
Chambersburg PA
CBHW021941160426
43195CB00011B/1179